AU TO BRITISH

A POCKET GUIDE TO TRANSLATING ENGLISH TO ENGLISH

So you don't look stupid when trying to understand Australian English words

PREFACE

Most people travelling to and from Australia don't expect there to be a language barrier but there are more differences in British vs Australian words than you think. This mini illustrated 'dictionary' is here to rescue you.

CHEERS!

A COLD ONE

BEER

ALF

STUPID PERSON

AMBER

BEER

ANKLE BITER

CHILD

ARVO

AFTERNOON

AUSTRALIAN

AUSSIE

AVO

AVOCADO

BACK OF BOURKE

MIDDLE OF NOWHERE

BARBIE

BARBEQUE

BATHERS

SWIMMING COSTUME

BELT UP

SHUT UP

BERKO

ANGRY

BIKKIE

BISCUIT

BILLIE

KETTLE

BIRO

BALL-POINT PEN

BONZA

BRILLIANT

BOTTLE O

OFF-LICENCE

BOTTLE SHOP

OFF-LICENCE

BRUCE

AUSTRALIAN MAN

BUSH

FOREST

BUSHRANGER

CRIMINAL

BUSHWALKING

HIKING

CACTUS

BROKEN

CHALKIE

TEACHER

CHOKKIE

CHOCOLATE

CHOOK

CHICKEN

CHRISSIE

CHRISTMAS

COMFORT STATION

TOILET

CUT LUNCH

SANDWICHES

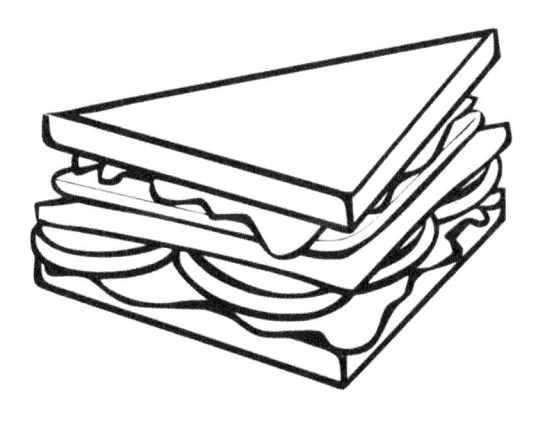

DAKS

TROUSERS

DAMPER

BREAD

DEADSET

TRUE

DIGGER

SOLDIER

DONK

CAR ENGINE

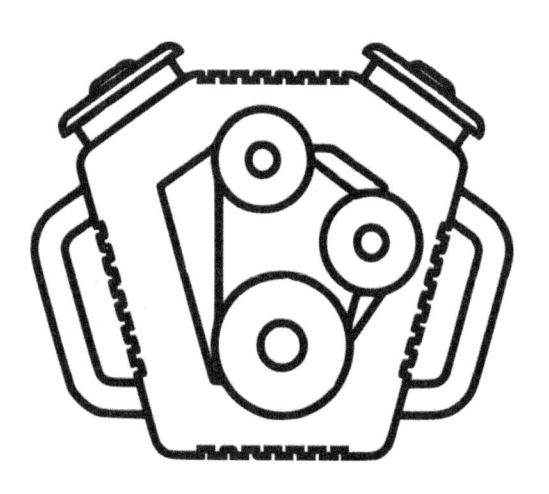

DRONGO

IDIOT

DUNNY

TOILET

FLAKE

SHARK MEAT

GANDER

HAVE A LOOK

GARBO

DUSTBIN MAN

G'DAY MATE

HELLO

GIVE AWAY

GIVE UP

GOOD LURK

GOOD JOB

GOOD OIL

EXACT INFORMATION

GOOD ON YA

WELL DONE

GRIZZLE

COMPLAIN

GROG

ALCOHOL

HEAPS

MANY

HOON

HOOLIGAN

HOW ARE YOU GOING?

HOW ARE YOU?

JACKAROO

CATTLE FARM TRAINEE

JOCKS

PANTS

JOE BLAKE

SNAKE

KELPIE

SHEEP DOG

KIWI

NEW ZEALANDER

LOLLIES

SWEETS

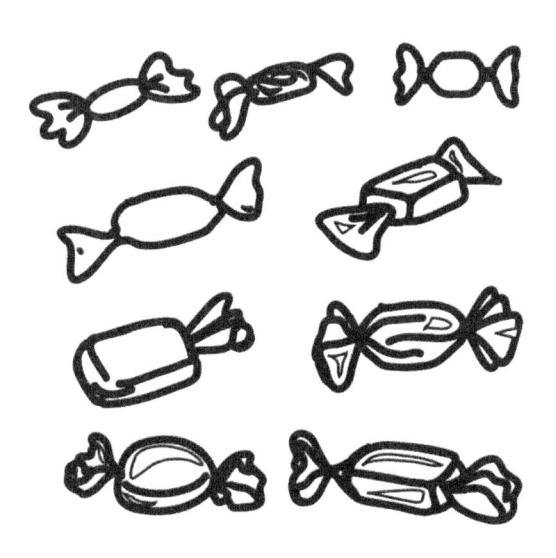

LOLLY

MONEY

MACCAS

MCDONALDS

MANCHESTER

BED LINEN

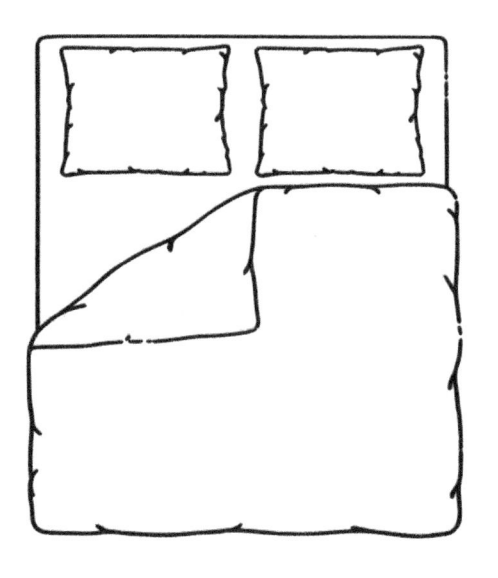

MILKO

MILKMAN

MORTICIAN

UNDERTAKER

MOZZIE

MOSQUITO

NANA

BANANA

NEDDIES

HORSES

NO WUCKAS

NO WORRIES

NUDDY

NAKED

OIL

INFORMATION

PASH

KISS

PIFFLE

NONESENSE

PLONK

CHEAP WINE

POM

ENGLISH PERSON

POSTIE

POSTMAN

POT

BEER GLASS

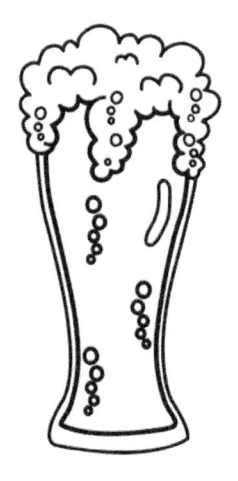

POWER POINT

SOCKET

PRANG

ACCIDENT

RACK OFF

GO AWAY

RAPT

VERY HAPPY

REAL ESTATE AGENT

ESTATE AGENT

RECKON

ABSOLUTELY

RELLIES

RELATIVES

RIGHTIO

OK

ROO

KANGAROO

ROOTED

TIRED

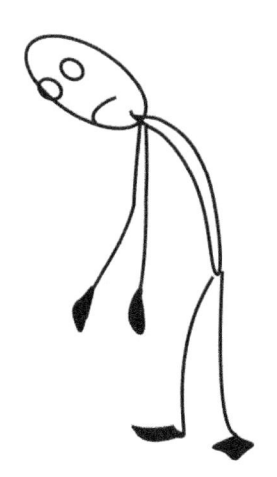

ROOTED

WORN OUT

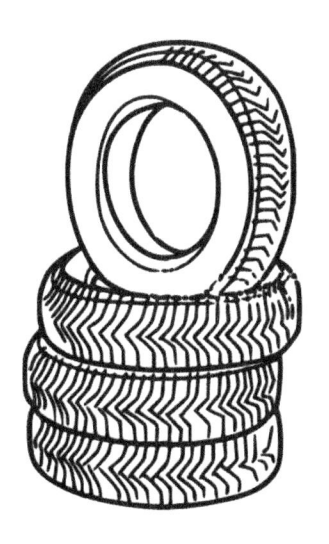

RUNNERS

TRAINERS

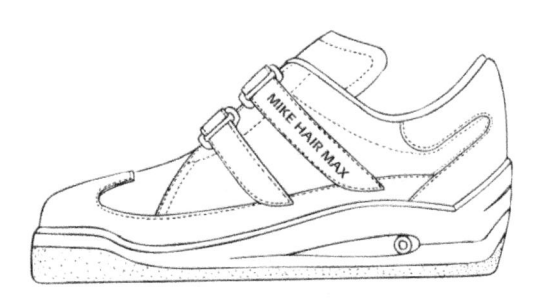

SACKED

FIRED

SERVO

GARAGE

SHEILA

WOMAN

SHOVE OFF

GO AWAY

SMOKO

CIGARETTE BREAK

SNAG

SAUSAGE

SNAKES HISS

PEE

STATION

FARM

STRALIA

AUSTRALIA

STRIDES

TROUSERS

SUNBAKE

SUNBATHE

SUNNIES

SUNGLASSES

TUCKER

FOOD

U-IE

U-TURN

UTE

SUV

VEGGIES

VEGETABLES

WOOL GROWER

SHEPHERD

YANK

AMERICAN

YONKS

LONG TIME

YOU BEAUTY

GREAT